# STRUGGLE for a CONTINENT

## The French and Indian Wars ★ 1689–1763

*by* **Betsy Maestro**

*Illustrated by* **Giulio Maestro**

HarperCollins*Publishers*

*Title page illustration:*
*Québec in 1761, after capture by the British*

Pen and ink, watercolor and colored pencil were used for the full-color illustrations.
The text type is 14-point ITC Garamond Book.

Struggle for a Continent: The French and Indian Wars 1689–1763
Text copyright © 2000 by Betsy Maestro
Illustrations copyright © 2000 by Giulio Maestro

Printed in Singapore at Tien Wah Press. All rights reserved.
www.harperchildrens.com

Library of Congress Cataloging-in-Publication Data
Maestro, Betsy.
Struggle for a continent: the French and Indian Wars, 1689–1763/Betsy and Giulio Maestro.
p.  cm.
Includes index.
Summary: Discusses the relations between the European colonists and the Native Americans,
the disputes between settlers from France, England, and Spain, and the role these conflicts
played in the history of North America.
ISBN 0-688-13450-5 (trade)—ISBN 0-688-13451-3 (library)
1. United States—History, Military—To 1900—Juvenile literature.  2. United States—History—
King William's War, 1689–1697—Juvenile literature.   3. United States—History—Queen Anne's War,
1702–1713—Juvenile literature.   4. United States—History—King George's War, 1744–1748—Juvenile
literature.  5. United States—History—French and Indian War, 1755–1763—Juvenile literature.
[1. United States—History—Colonial period, ca. 1600–1775. 2. United States—History—
French and Indian War, 1755–1763.]  I. Maestro, Giulio.  II. Title.
E195.M25 2000   973.2'5—dc21   99-11500   CIP

2  4  6  8  10  9  7  5  3
❖
First Edition

NORTH AMERICA IS A HUGE CONTINENT ENCOMPASSING thousands of square miles—from the Atlantic to the Pacific, from Canada to Mexico. After the voyages of Christopher Columbus and John Cabot, European countries became interested in what this vast continent might offer them. As early as 1630, Spain, France, England, and the Netherlands had settlements in North America. These European nations were ruled by kings and queens who were always looking for ways to expand their territory beyond existing borders and across the oceans of the world. Constantly at war with one another over trade, borders, and religious disputes, these rival nations challenged one another on land and at sea. Beginning in 1689, the conflicts in Europe spread across the Atlantic to America. Over the next seventy years, competing European powers would struggle for a continent. The winner would take the prize—all of North America.

*A battle between French and English ships, around 1700*

By the year 1689, the Netherlands and Spain were out of the contest. The Dutch had been forced to surrender their territory to the English; and the Spanish, after a number of unsuccessful expeditions, had chosen to limit their interests to their missions in Florida and New Spain, in what is now Mexico. So it was England and France that were left to do battle over the rest of North America.

The French and the English had vastly different plans for the future of North America. The French saw the continent as a profitable fur-trading empire. They hoped to extend the borders of New France to include all of the land between the Great Lakes in the north and the Gulf of Mexico in the south, and between the St. Lawrence River in the east and the Rocky Mountains in the west. The French dreamed of traveling inland on the highways of the wilderness—the great rivers that led west to the Pacific Ocean—to gain control of the whole continent.

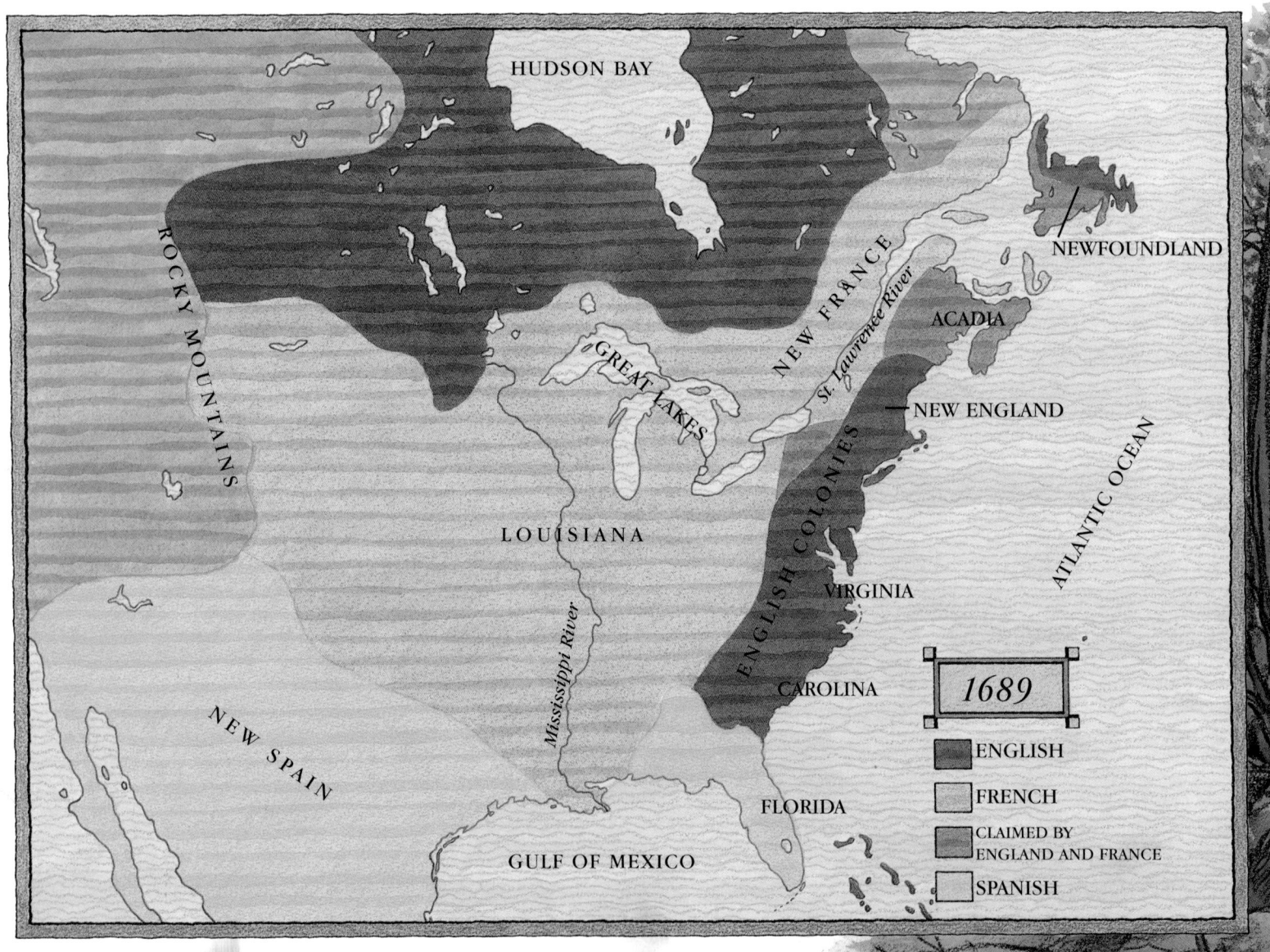

*English fishermen along the New England coast*

Great Britain had another view of the future of North America. The English king and his government saw their colonies in America as a permanent home for all those who were not content with life in England—a perfect place to send troublemakers. The colonies would also provide profitable trading opportunities. Immigration to the "New World" was encouraged, and the poor and oppressed grasped at the chance to find prosperity and religious freedom in America. By 1664, England controlled the Atlantic seacoast between New France (now Canada) in the north and Spanish Florida in the south. Twenty-five years later, in 1689, there were more than two hundred thousand English settlers in the North American colonies.

By comparison, the French population of New France was very small—about ten thousand adventurers, traders, explorers, and priests widely scattered in what is now eastern Canada. The French king had done little to encourage settlement in America, and those who had come were mostly men. There were few French families in New France.

*French traders haul a canoe through the rapids.*

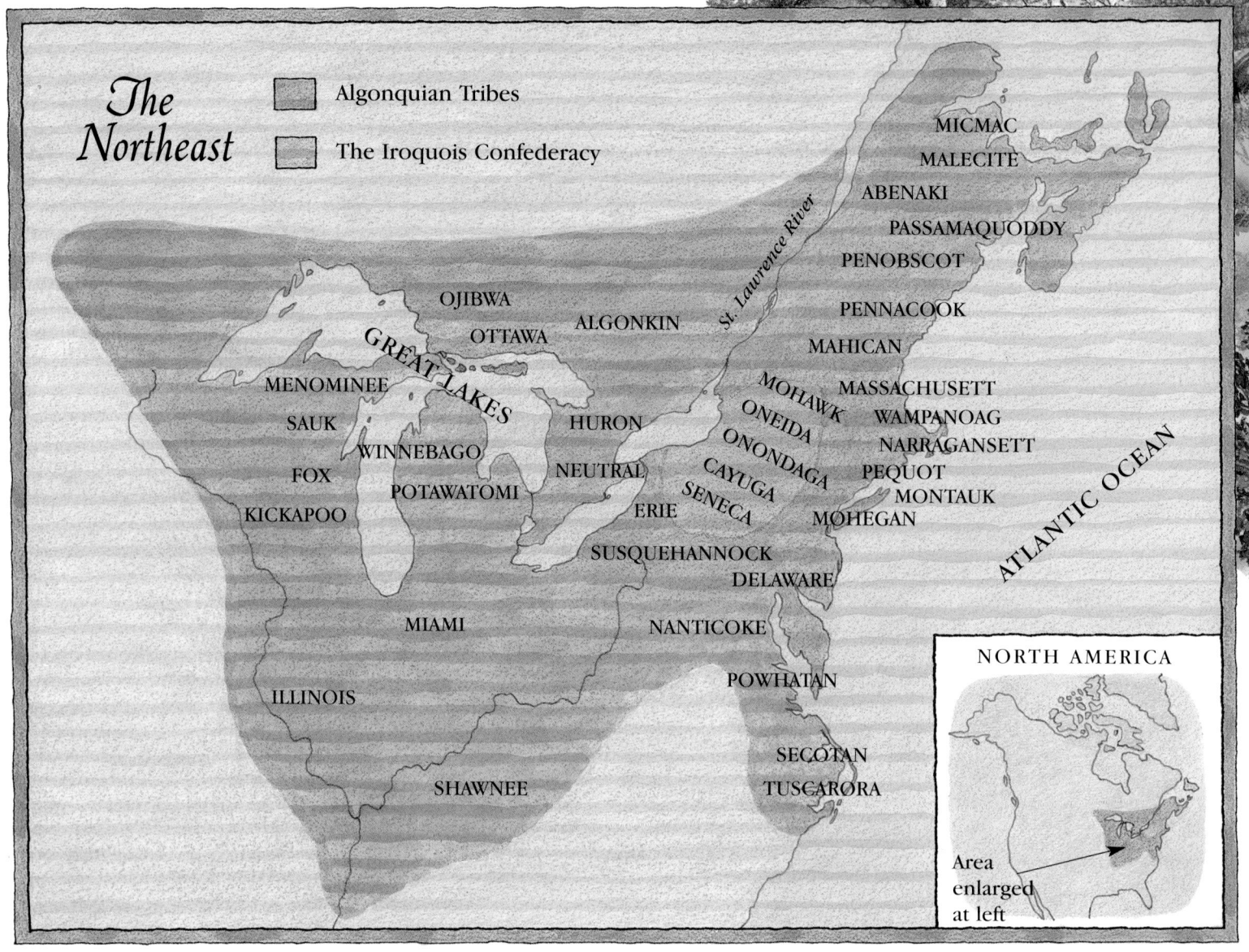

The Northeast

*Algonquian Tribes*
*The Iroquois Confederacy*

MICMAC
MALECITE
ABENAKI
PASSAMAQUODDY
PENOBSCOT
PENNACOOK
MAHICAN
OJIBWA
OTTAWA
ALGONKIN
St. Lawrence River
MASSACHUSETT
MOHAWK
ONEIDA
WAMPANOAG
MENOMINEE
GREAT LAKES
HURON
ONONDAGA
NARRAGANSETT
SAUK
CAYUGA
PEQUOT
WINNEBAGO
NEUTRAL
SENECA
MONTAUK
FOX
POTAWATOMI
ERIE
MOHEGAN
KICKAPOO
SUSQUEHANNOCK
DELAWARE
ATLANTIC OCEAN
MIAMI
NANTICOKE
POWHATAN
ILLINOIS
SECOTAN
TUSCARORA
SHAWNEE

NORTH AMERICA

Area enlarged at left

North America had a much larger population that was neither French nor English. There were more than a million Native Americans—called Indians by the Europeans—in the large area that now makes up the United States and Canada. No one knows for sure, but there were probably about three hundred thousand Indians living in or near the areas of French and English settlement.

Most of the Indians in the Northeast belonged to one of two large groups—the Algonquian tribes or the Iroquoian tribes—that were related by similar lifeways and languages. The Algonquian tribes lived in a very widespread area that included the Great Lakes as well as the Atlantic coast, while most of the Iroquoian tribes lived more closely together in what is now central New York State.

*Algonquian wigwams*

Both groups were woodland Indians who hunted, fished, farmed, and traded. They lived in family groups within larger community groups and were strongly loyal to both family and tribe. Women played an important role in tribal leadership in the Northeast, and they were solely responsible for raising crops. While the Iroquois resided in long communal dwellings called longhouses, most Algonquians lived in wigwams.

The Iroquoian tribes—the Mohawk, Seneca, Oneida, Cayuga, and Onondaga—had formed a strong alliance. These Five Nations had pledged to come together as one for the protection of all. This union made the Iroquois very powerful—they were both feared and respected by the Algonquian tribes scattered throughout the region.

*An Iroquois longhouse*

In the Northeast, the early contacts between Europeans and Indians had been mostly friendly and cooperative. At Jamestown and at Plymouth, English settlers owed their lives to the kindness and teachings of their native neighbors. But later, when large numbers of new Americans arrived, they pushed the Indians off their hunting lands, and relations became strained and hostile. In New England, conflicts between Indians and English settlers erupted several times into warfare. The Indians were always the losers in these conflicts, where they were mostly outnumbered and underarmed.

The French, on the other hand, had long enjoyed friendly relations with most of the Algonquian-speaking tribes of the northern woodlands. French traders had lived among the Indians for many years and had learned their ways and their languages, which led them to respect native traditions and skills. The French treated the Indians as valuable trading partners and relied on their cooperation as guides, advisers, and mapmakers. Without the help of the Huron, Ottawa, and Ojibwa, there would have been no fur trade.

*French fur traders in winter*

In New York's Hudson Valley, the Dutch had arranged a very successful trading relationship with the Iroquois. In 1664, when the English officially took control of the area, they inherited this valuable Indian partnership. Europeans had come to North America to open new trading opportunities, and they soon discovered the most profitable treasure of the continent— fur. Very quickly, the fur trade became an enormous financial success. Beaver pelts, used to make popular felt hats in Europe, brought in huge profits for traders, trading companies, and governments.

The Iroquois were not content with their share of this profitable trade. For years, the French and their Algonquian allies had dominated most of the fur trade, and the Iroquois resented their success. Beginning in about 1649, the Iroquois waged wars of terror on the Algonquian tribes to the north. Many Algonquian tribes were defeated during the relentless attacks of the Beaver Wars. The Iroquois victories, over more than thirty years, allowed them to carve out a larger trading region of their own, from the Ottawa River in the north to the Cumberland River in the south, and from Lake Ontario eastward to Maine.

*At dawn, Algonquians are awakened by the approach of Iroquois war canoes.*

*Beaver*                                                    *Fox*

Trade was the main reason for cooperation between the Indians and the Europeans. The Indians had a long history of trading with one another to obtain essential items that they could not make or get themselves. Corn, beans, and squash could be traded for animal skins and meat. But the arrival of the Europeans brought many changes in the Indian way of life. Indian habits and customs were altered by the easy availability of European goods, such as knives, iron tools and pots, fine cloth and blankets, and one particular product that they now could not do without—guns. Many tribes had replaced their own weapons—used in both hunting and warfare—with European firearms and ammunition. The Indians relied on the fur trade for resupply.

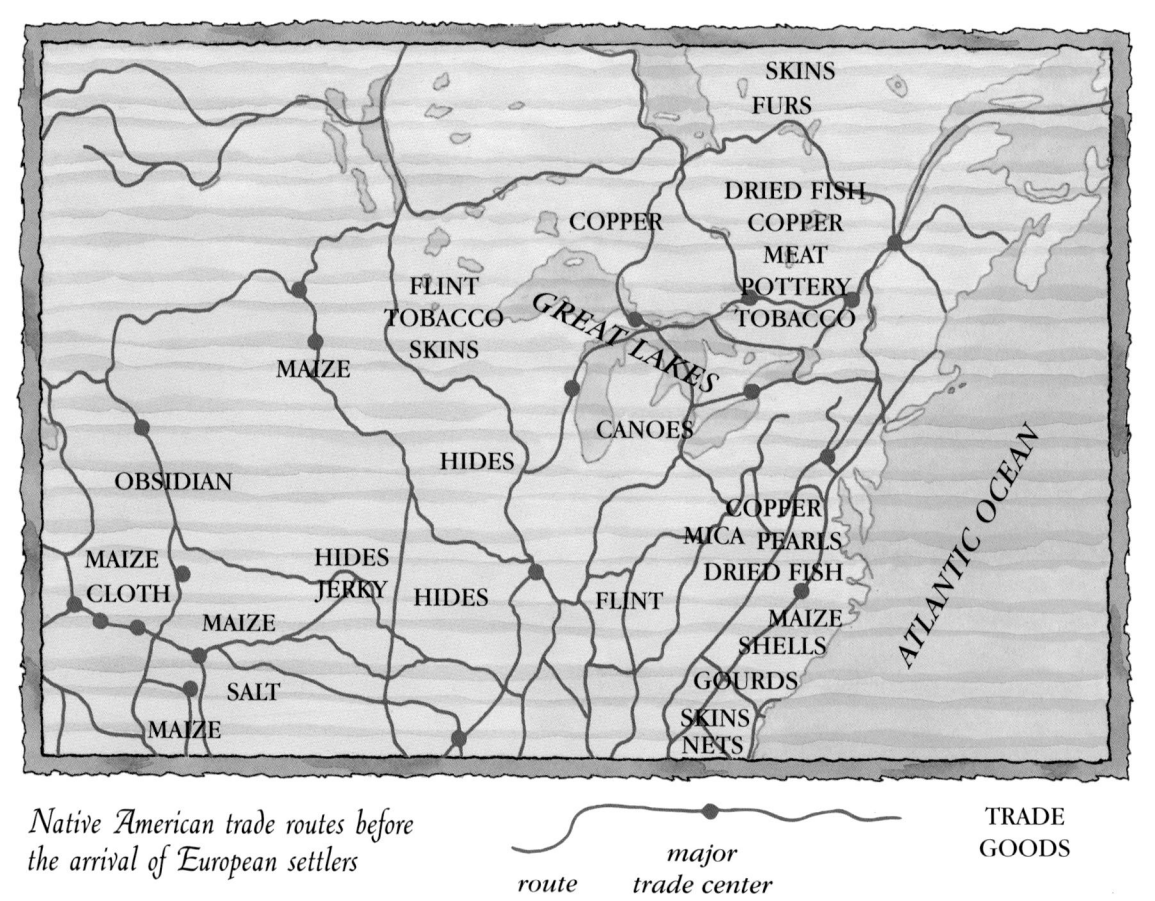

*Native American trade routes before the arrival of European settlers*

route — major trade center

TRADE GOODS

Lynx

River Otter

The French and the English both used the Indians' dependence on guns and ammunition to their own advantage. The promise of a continuous supply of weapons was often enough to enlist Indian help in the white men's wars. Indian tribal groups in the Northeast were widely scattered over huge areas of coastline, woodlands, and mountains. Except for the Iroquois, these groups were not part of one united nation, but were instead like many small independent nations loosely held together by treaties. For each of these small nations, tribal identity—pride and a sense of belonging to their group—was stronger than their feelings for other Indian nations, or for all Native Americans as one huge nation. As a result, tribal groups easily sided with their white trading partners against unrelated or enemy tribes. They looked to their European or colonial allies to help protect their territory and trade, and they sometimes used the white men's wars as a way of settling old scores with their own enemies.

European trade goods

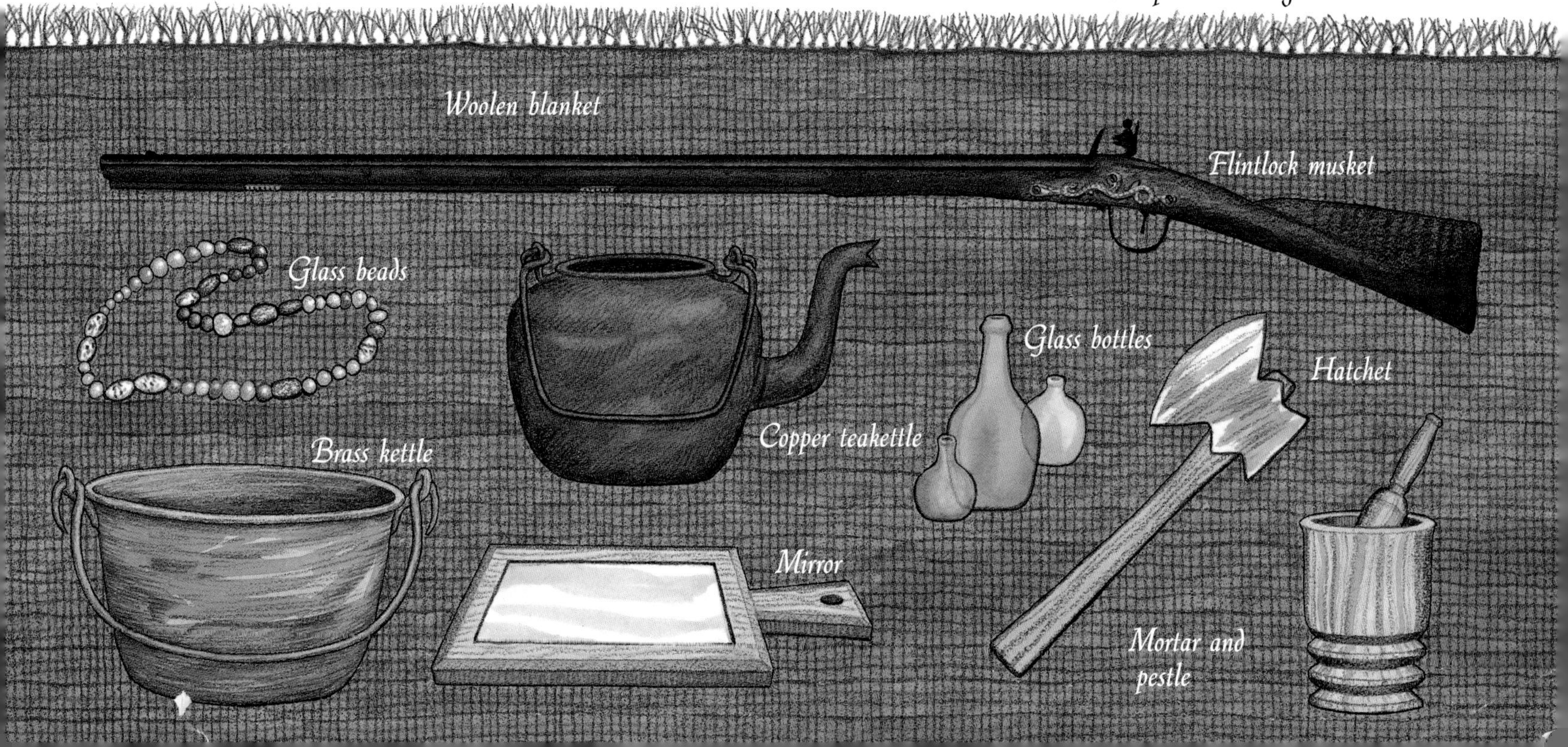

Woolen blanket

Flintlock musket

Glass beads

Copper teakettle

Glass bottles

Hatchet

Brass kettle

Mirror

Mortar and pestle

The struggle between the French and the English was very much like the struggle between the Iroquois and the Algonquians—a struggle for land and trade. Because the French did not force Indians to give up their land, they had many willing Indian allies against the English. The Indians trusted and befriended the French, since over time they had proved to be fair and honest traders. In turn, the Indians taught the French to become skilled woodsmen, who could fight and survive in the wilderness.

Although widely separated by vast distances, the citizens of New France were united in their loyalty to the French king, and in the years to come they readily gave their lives for the French cause. However, their numbers were small when compared to those of their English counterparts to the south.

*A French settlement along the St. Lawrence River, around 1689*

The population of the English colonies, at about two hundred thousand, was more than twenty times the French population of New France. This was a big advantage, but it was balanced by a number of disadvantages. The English colonists, like the French, were scattered over large areas and often quite isolated from one another. The problems of New England farmers were not very important to plantation owners in the Carolinas or Virginia. In addition, most English colonists were farmers or merchants—unskilled in the ways of the wilderness—who would not be much of a match for French woodsmen. But these colonial settlers were a hardy group; they would help their king when called upon, and they would most certainly rise up to protect their homes and land. And they too would have Indian help. Their trading partners, the Iroquois, needed little encouragement to help in the fight against the French and their Algonquian allies.

The long struggle between France and England, known in America as the French and Indian Wars, was not, as the name suggests, wars between the French and the Indians. The fighting was between the French and Algonquian Indians on one side and the English and the Iroquois on the other. The American conflicts were closely related to the wars in Europe between France, England, Spain, and the Netherlands. Each time war broke out in Europe, the effects were felt around the world wherever these rival nations had colonies or trading posts. The kings and queens of Europe expected their loyal subjects to fight for their causes no matter where they were. In North America, the French and English colonists used these European wars as an excuse to start their own battles over land and trade, and both sides needed Indian help.

*Trade routes in the late 1600s*

*Algonquian/French*  *Iroquois/English*

Serious trouble began in the area of New York's Appalachian Mountains over access to the fur trade. The French controlled an open highway to the Great Lakes and the fur supply—the St. Lawrence River. The English and the Iroquois used two trade routes beginning in the Hudson River, one that went west to Lake Ontario, and one that went north to the St. Lawrence. Although both of these routes were long and difficult to travel, with many portages, or overland stretches, between the lakes and rivers, they did allow the English and the Iroquois to compete with the French. Many times the French tried to cut off these routes, but each time, the English and the Iroquois reopened them.

In 1687, the frustrated French sent an army of settlers and Algonquian allies south into New York to attack Iroquois villages. In retaliation, on a summer night in 1689, Iroquois warriors raided the French village of Lachine, near Montréal. The settlement was left to burn, its two hundred residents murdered in the swift attack.

*French and Indians attacking an Iroquois village*

*The attack on Schenectady, 1690*

The first of the French and Indian Wars—called King William's War, after the English king—began in 1689. In Europe, France and England went to war, and although neither nation sent soldiers to fight the war in America, they encouraged their colonists to protect the interests of their kings. The governor of New France ordered attacks on towns in New York and the New England colonies. On a winter night in 1690, the French and Algonquians crossed over the ice of Lake Champlain and destroyed the small settlement of Schenectady, New York. The war party massacred or kidnapped all of the settlers. This was the first of many such raids in New York, Maine, New Hampshire, and Connecticut.

Port Royal

The English colonists and the Iroquois fought back, staging similar attacks on villages along the borders of New France. But the slaughter of so many settlers and the frequency of French and Indian raids created fear and panic throughout New York and New England. Massachusetts colonists planned revenge. They set out in fourteen boats to challenge the French at Port Royal in Acadia, now part of Nova Scotia. Their success in this venture encouraged them to mount an attack on the French city of Québec. This assault was doomed to failure, as the walled city high above the St. Lawrence River was well protected.

King William's War ended with the signing of a peace treaty in 1697. All captured territory was returned, and neither France nor England gained anything from all the fighting and loss of life. Nothing had been resolved.

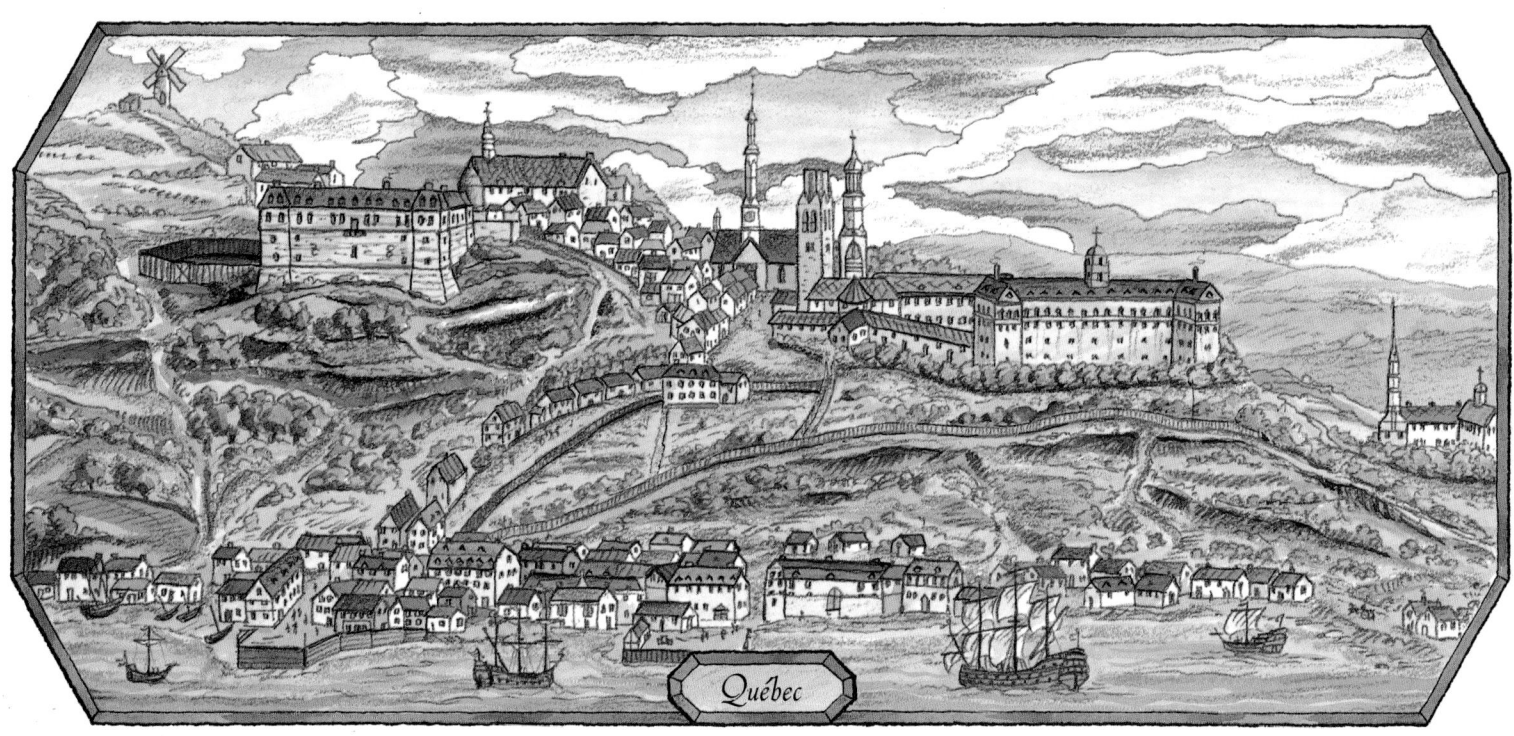

Québec

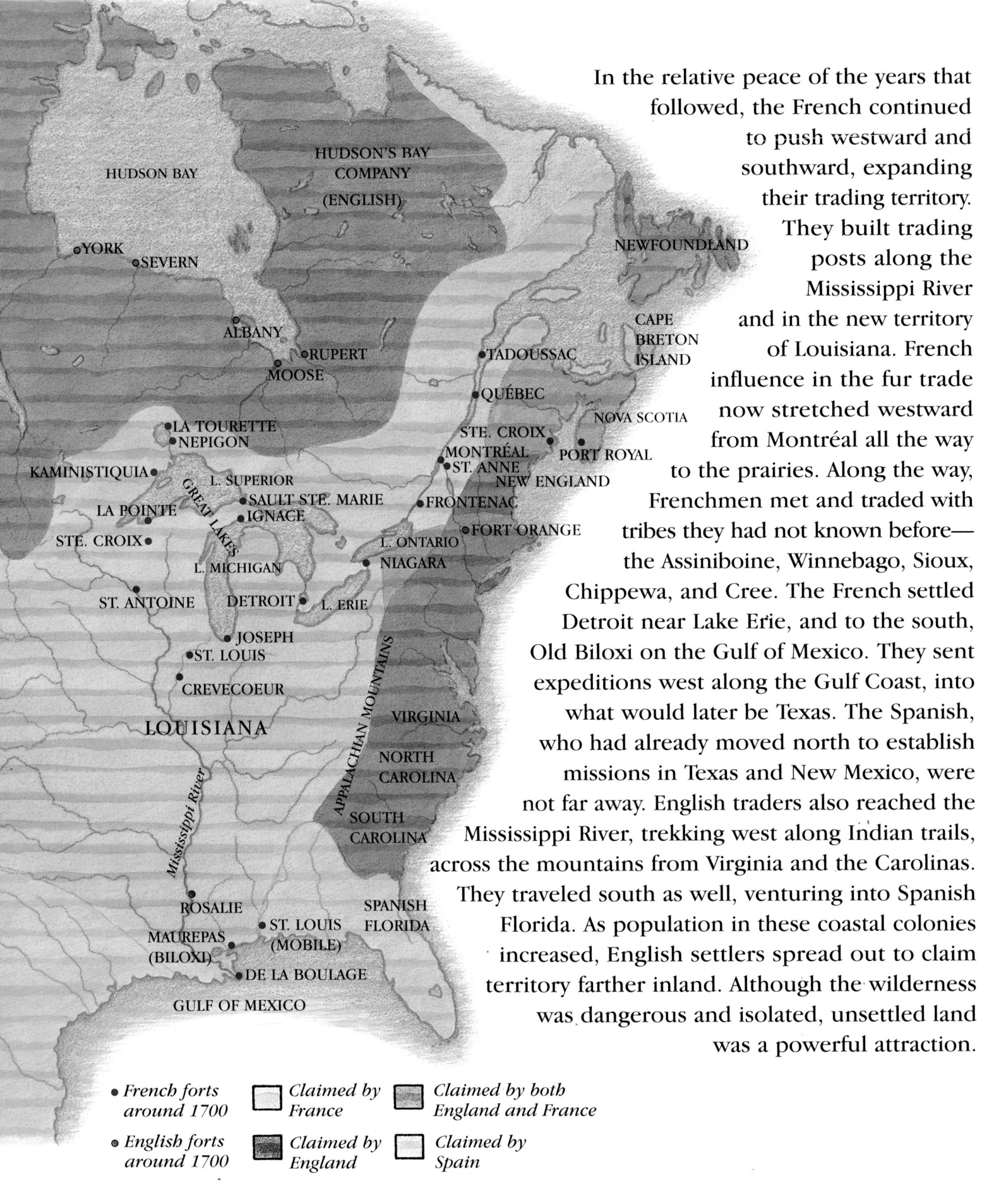

In the relative peace of the years that followed, the French continued to push westward and southward, expanding their trading territory. They built trading posts along the Mississippi River and in the new territory of Louisiana. French influence in the fur trade now stretched westward from Montréal all the way to the prairies. Along the way, Frenchmen met and traded with tribes they had not known before—the Assiniboine, Winnebago, Sioux, Chippewa, and Cree. The French settled Detroit near Lake Erie, and to the south, Old Biloxi on the Gulf of Mexico. They sent expeditions west along the Gulf Coast, into what would later be Texas. The Spanish, who had already moved north to establish missions in Texas and New Mexico, were not far away. English traders also reached the Mississippi River, trekking west along Indian trails, across the mountains from Virginia and the Carolinas. They traveled south as well, venturing into Spanish Florida. As population in these coastal colonies increased, English settlers spread out to claim territory farther inland. Although the wilderness was dangerous and isolated, unsettled land was a powerful attraction.

Map labels: HUDSON BAY, HUDSON'S BAY COMPANY (ENGLISH), NEWFOUNDLAND, YORK, SEVERN, ALBANY, RUPERT, MOOSE, TADOUSSAC, CAPE BRETON ISLAND, QUÉBEC, NOVA SCOTIA, LA TOURETTE, NEPIGON, STE. CROIX, MONTRÉAL, PORT ROYAL, ST. ANNE, NEW ENGLAND, KAMINISTIQUIA, L. SUPERIOR, SAULT STE. MARIE, FRONTENAC, LA POINTE, IGNACE, FORT ORANGE, STE. CROIX, L. ONTARIO, NIAGARA, GREAT LAKES, L. MICHIGAN, ST. ANTOINE, DETROIT, L. ERIE, JOSEPH, ST. LOUIS, CREVECOEUR, APPALACHIAN MOUNTAINS, VIRGINIA, LOUISIANA, Mississippi River, NORTH CAROLINA, SOUTH CAROLINA, ROSALIE, SPANISH FLORIDA, MAUREPAS (BILOXI), ST. LOUIS (MOBILE), DE LA BOULAGE, GULF OF MEXICO

Legend:
- French forts around 1700
- English forts around 1700
- Claimed by France
- Claimed by England
- Claimed by both England and France
- Claimed by Spain

Far to the north, in the icy regions of Hudson Bay, the English had constructed a series of forts to protect their fur-trading interests. They traded with Indians, who often trudged hundreds of miles through bitter cold to bring them furs. These skins would then be shipped out of Hudson Bay directly to England. A little to the south, the French had forts all around the Great Lakes to protect their area of the fur trade. The fierce competition between these two groups for Indian alliances and furs led to a long series of raids and counterraids in this northern area for more than thirty years. The extreme overhunting of the beaver almost led to its extinction.

As the competition grew, hostilities among rival traders, colonists, and Indians increased despite the official peace between 1697 and 1702. The French and Spanish became increasingly alarmed at the challenges to their land claims and trade as the English frontier slowly moved west and south.

*Fort Detroit*

*Charles Town (later Charleston) harbor, around 1700*

Life in many places in the English colonies was unaffected by the skirmishes along the frontier. By the start of the new century, such American cities as Boston, New York, Philadelphia, Charleston, Newport, and Williamsburg had grown to become important centers of trade and shipping, as well as seats of colonial government. Farms and plantations, mills and fisheries, shipyards and ironworks were busy producing the food and products needed for use in the colonies and for trade with England. By 1700, nearly every town in New England that had a river or stream also had a busy sawmill providing lumber for the expanding colonies.

For most, life in America felt more secure—there was safety in numbers, and now there were about two hundred seventy-five thousand people in the twelve colonies along the Atlantic coast. With the arrival of settlers from Scotland and Ireland, Germany and Switzerland, Sweden and Finland, and even France—French Protestants, called Huguenots—life in the "English" colonies became more diverse. The new settlers brought with them great variety in lifestyles, religious practices, and customs, which contributed to an atmosphere of tolerance, freedom, and democracy that was replacing the narrow Puritan views of earlier years.

*A New England farm and sawmill*

But there were people living in the English colonies who did not enjoy freedom or tolerance. By 1700, there were about twenty-eight thousand African slaves in the colonies. Most were put to work on southern plantations, but slavery was present in the North as well. New England shipowners were actively engaged in the slave trade, bringing slaves from Africa on American ships.

Africans were not the only ones to be kidnapped and forced into slavery. Slave traders in the Carolinas sent their Indian allies into the interior with guns to capture Indians of enemy tribes. These native-born Americans were sold into slavery in the West Indies, and some tribes, such as the Timucua in Florida, were wiped out completely by this brutal trade. These activities did not win Indian friends for the English, and many tribes turned to the French for protection.

*A slave auction, around 1700*

*Settlers captured at Deerfield*

In 1701, war began again in Europe, with Great Britain and its allies—including Portugal and the Netherlands—fighting against France and Spain. A year later, the conflict broke out in North America, where it was called Queen Anne's War.

The French and Algonquians resumed their reign of terror along the New England frontier. One of the worst attacks was mounted in Deerfield, Massachusetts, in the winter of 1704. About two hundred and fifty Abenaki Indians and French settlers attacked the stockaded town, striking just before dawn, when the inhabitants were asleep. The raiding Indians slew fifty colonists in their beds, and more than a hundred others were captured and marched north through the snow toward Canada. Some died or were killed on the way, and others were held for ransom or adopted by the Indians.

The frontier raids—the attacks and counterattacks—that occurred during these wars were brutal. Torture and scalpings were often carried out by both sides. Religious intolerance led French priests to organize Indian raids on English Protestant settlements, while New England preachers encouraged attacks on Catholic villages in Canada.

In 1703, Carolina colonists looted and burned Spanish settlements in Florida. A few years later, they managed to turn back an attack launched from Spanish and French ships off the coast of Charleston.

A large expedition of English forces was sent to fight the French in Canada in 1711. After recapturing Port Royal, they sailed toward Québec for another try at the French city. But during the foggy night, strong winds sent the ten ships crashing against the rocks, and more than one thousand sailors lost their lives.

Queen Anne's War came to an official end in 1713, when a new treaty formally declared all of French Acadia, Newfoundland, and Hudson Bay to be English territory. The French held on to Cape Breton Island and to the islands in the St. Lawrence River.

*The ill-fated English expedition of 1711*

Although North America was now at peace, the French were thinking of the future. They worried that England, with her newly gained territory, was in a strong position to cut off French access to the St. Lawrence River. New France could not survive without this important supply route to the interior. So France looked for a way to protect the entrance to the St. Lawrence. On Cape Breton Island, looking out to the sea, they built the great fortress of Louisbourg. From this secure lookout, they would hold a strong advantage over approaching British ships.

All the while, the French continued to move west and south on the continent, building new forts as they went. In the years ahead, they would be well prepared to defend their territory in the Mississippi Valley and along the Great Lakes and Lake Champlain.

*It took twenty-five years to complete the walled city of Louisbourg.*

Far to the south, in the Carolinas, the English colonists had no time to worry about the French. They had Indian uprisings on their hands. Tensions between a number of local tribes and the traders and settlers along the frontiers had grown. The Indians, who had been friendly to the colonists at first, became increasingly angry at the treatment they received. Traders gave the Indians liquor, then insulted and cheated them. Settlers took their best hunting lands without permission or payment, and slave traders kidnapped members of their tribes. The Indians rebelled. The uprisings were put down by colonial militia, and the Indians, as usual, were the losers. Surviving Tuscaroras, an Iroquoian tribe, were driven north, where they joined the Iroquois Confederacy. The Yamasees were almost totally wiped out in the fighting, and the few survivors fled to Florida. Carolina colonists quickly took over the Indian lands.

The nearby Spanish in Florida also worried the Carolina settlers. In 1733, King George II issued a charter establishing Georgia as the thirteenth English colony. Colonists hoped that Georgia would act as a buffer, protecting the Carolinas from the Spanish. General James Oglethorpe led more than one hundred colonists to what would later become Savannah.

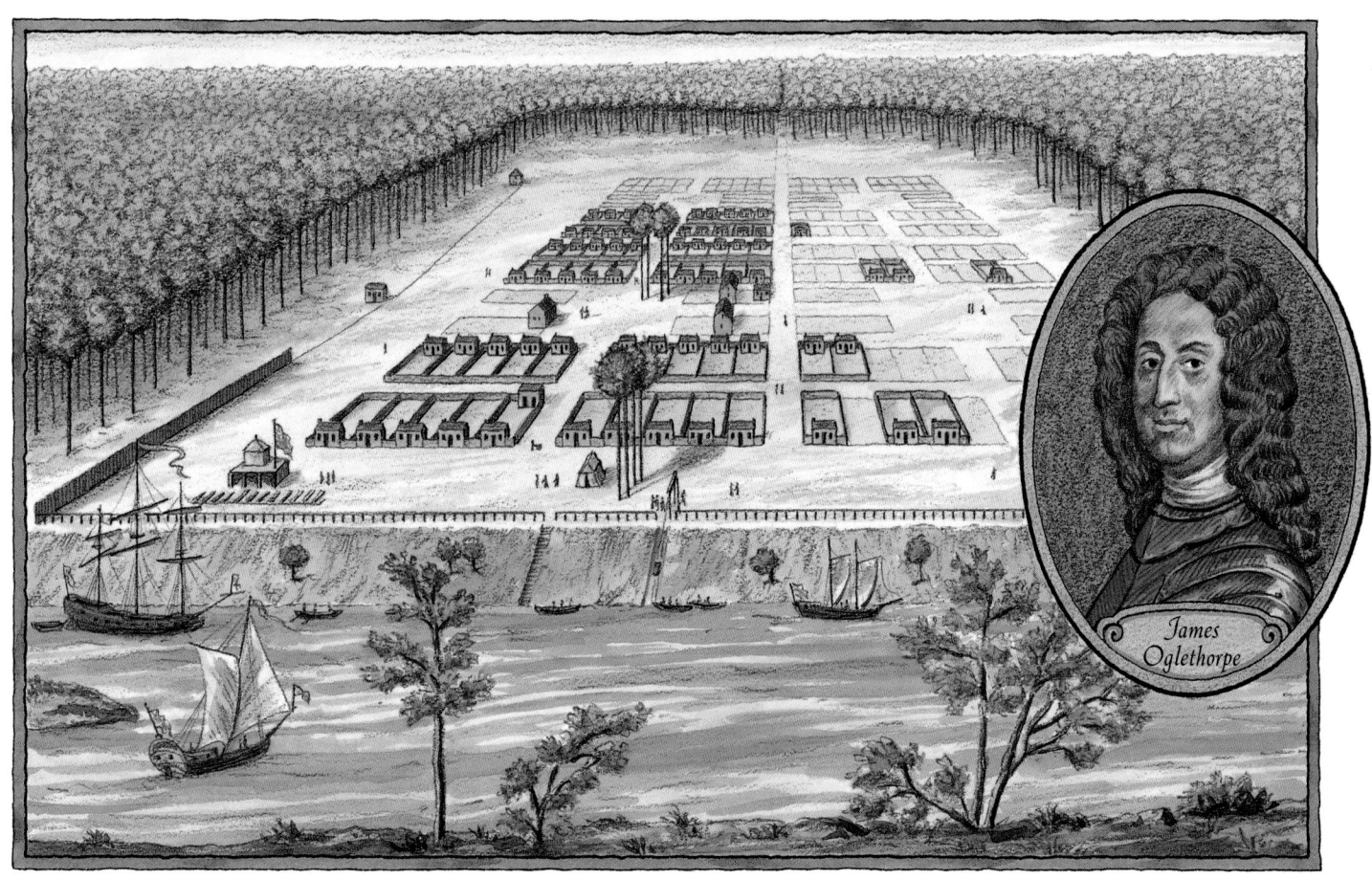

*Savannah under construction in 1734*

In 1739, a British sailor claimed that his ear had been cut off by the Spanish. This led to the War of Jenkins' Ear, between Spain and Great Britain. This small conflict grew into a bigger war when France joined Spain against England.

In North America, French and British colonists and soldiers again took up arms against each other in 1744, in what came to be called King George's War. Border settlements in New France, New York, and Massachusetts became easy targets once more, as Indians were drawn into the conflict yet again. The Iroquois felt threatened by French forces and their Algonquian allies, and they asked for British protection. The English built Fort Oswego on Lake Ontario, and the French countered by constructing a fort on Lake Champlain, which they could use to stage attacks on New York and New England.

But the main battle of the war was fought in Nova Scotia. After the French attacked the English in Acadia, New England colonists joined together to attempt the impossible—the capture of Louisbourg. This immense armed fortress and walled town on the tip of Cape Breton Island looked out onto the vast expanse of the Atlantic Ocean. Inside its massive stone walls lived about four thousand French men, women, and children. Only about seven hundred, however, were trained soldiers, not nearly enough to properly man all of the giant fort's cannons, guns, and lookouts.

*The French at Louisbourg*

Louisbourg Around 1740

Governor's Quarters and Barracks

Guardhouse

Armory

Laundry and Stables

Stables

Powder Magazine

Royal Storehouse

Artillery Storehouse

Gate

Barracks

Gate

In March of 1745, close to four thousand New Englanders sailed out of Boston Harbor in about one hundred boats and ships of assorted sizes. They were joined by British warships in the icy waters off Cape Breton. Toward the end of April, the army began landing a few miles from the mighty fortress. The shortage of French manpower had caused the abandonment of the Grand Battery facing the harbor. The large cannons left behind were painstakingly moved into new positions to fire upon the city of Louisbourg itself. The French were unprepared to defend themselves from this overland attack. The assault on Louisbourg took more than a month, but clever planning, determination, and good luck combined to bring about the French defeat.

*The British occupy the Grand Battery.*

New Englanders lost only about one hundred men in the actual battle, but more than a thousand died of sickness after the victory, during the many months they held the fort for the English. The following spring, they were at last relieved by British troops and could return home to their wives and children.

After this hard-fought victory, the colonists were furious with the terms of the new treaty that ended the war in 1748. England gave Louisbourg back to the French in exchange for territory in far-off India.

*British ships guard Louisbourg Harbor.*

*New England colonists move the huge French cannons into place.*

*The weekly post-rider*

*Philadelphia-to-New York stage wagons*

Even in the midst of warfare and struggle, life for most of the new Americans living in the English colonies was constantly changing for the better. As communication improved, the colonies became more united. With the establishment of a colonial postal system and the publication of more newspapers, people were more aware of what was happening in other colonies. Citizens in Boston began to feel more connected to other Americans in Virginia or the Carolinas.

As roads improved, so did transportation. Public stagecoach lines between big cities began to operate on regular schedules. In the middle of the 1700s, two new vehicles were put into use in Pennsylvania—the flatboat and the Conestoga wagon.

*A Conestoga wagon*

*A flatboat*

*Early Baltimore*

As the population grew, new cities were founded. Earlier in the 1700s, the city of New Orleans had been settled by immigrants from Canada and France, and the Spanish had founded the city of San Antonio in what is now Texas. A new city in the English colonies—Baltimore—had been established in 1730. Life in the bigger cities became safer with the installation of streetlights and the addition of police and fire protection. The introduction of sewers and garbage collection made cities cleaner and healthier as well.

Higher education flourished at seven colleges, including Harvard, Yale, and Princeton. Cultural activities blossomed as people had more time and money to enjoy them. Theaters and bookstores opened in some of the larger cities, and the first symphony orchestra was organized by the Moravian community in Pennsylvania in 1741. The colonists in North America wanted nothing more than to go on with their lives in continued peace and security. But trouble was brewing again, this time in a new area—the Ohio Valley.

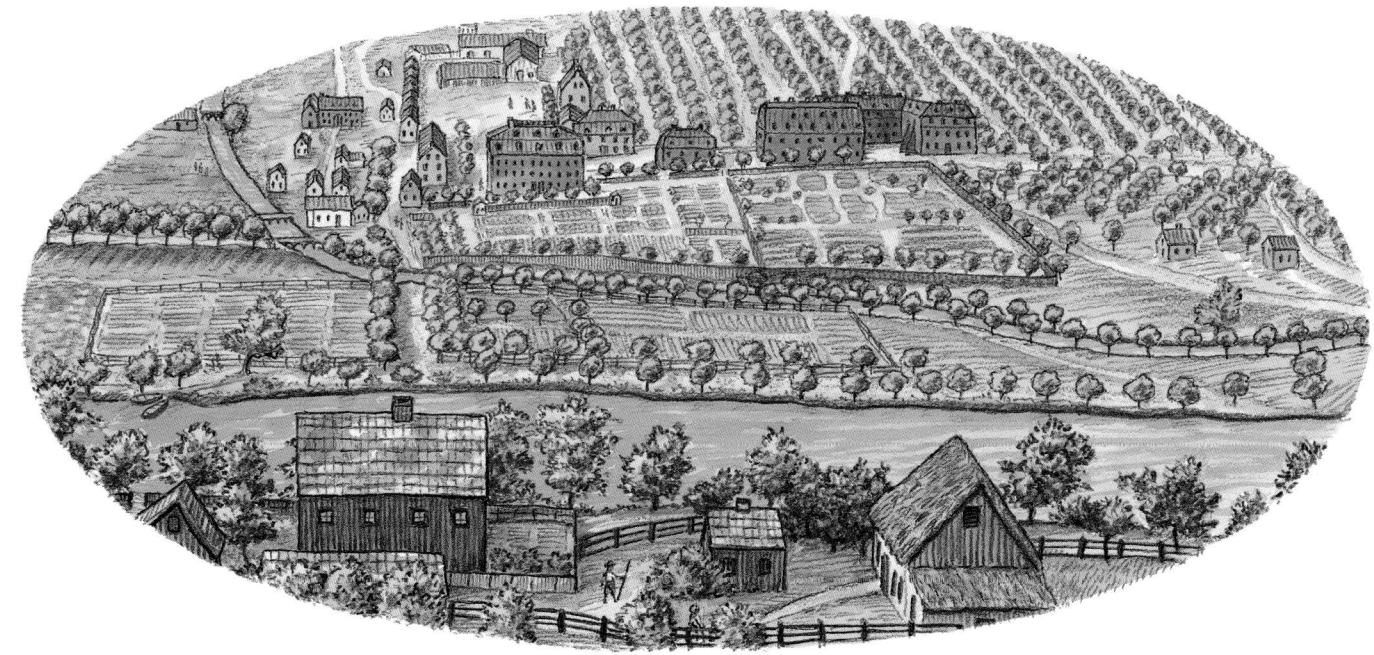

*Moravian settlement at Bethlehem, Pennsylvania*

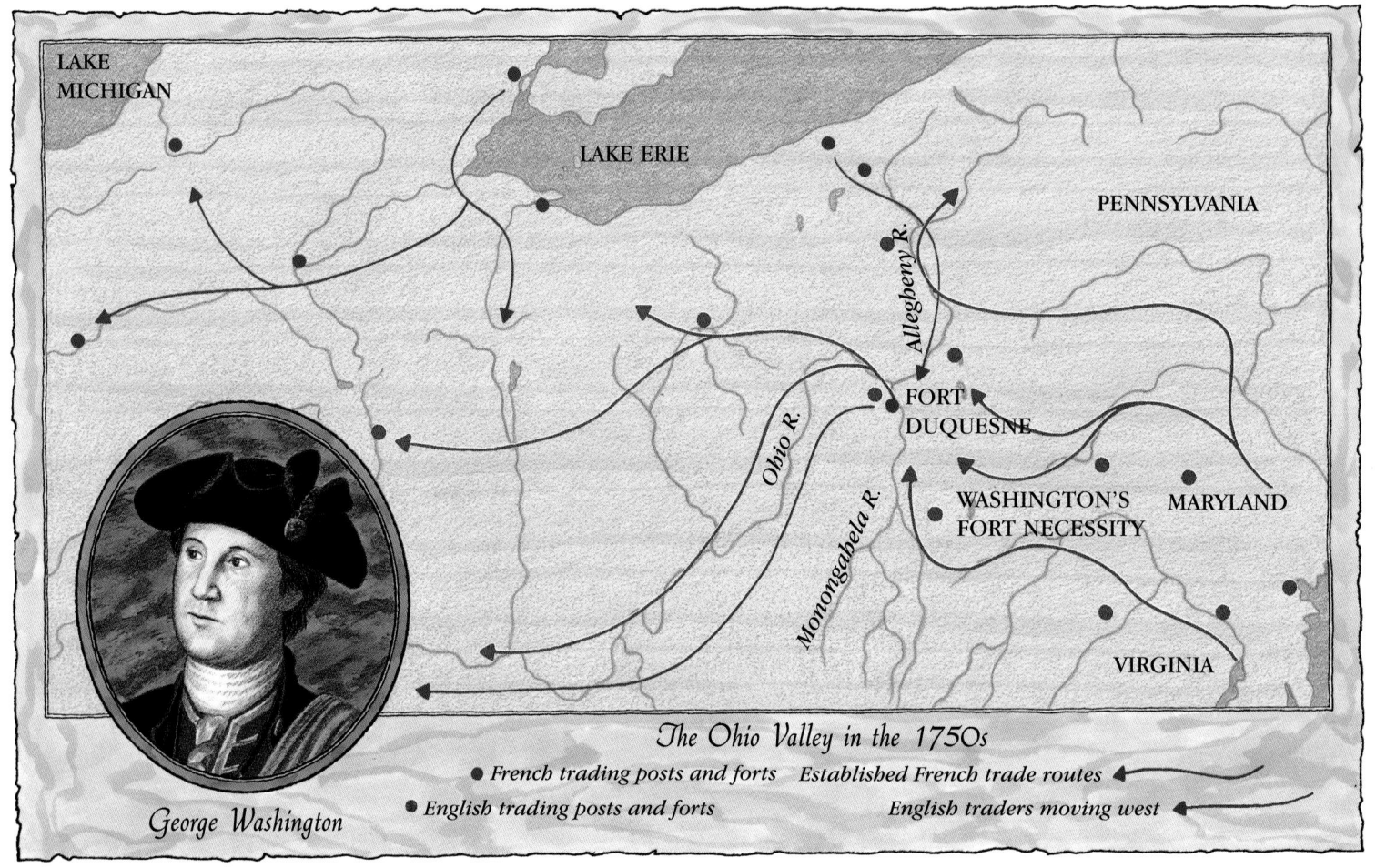

LAKE MICHIGAN

LAKE ERIE

PENNSYLVANIA

*Allegheny R.*

*Ohio R.*

FORT DUQUESNE

*Monongahela R.*

WASHINGTON'S FORT NECESSITY

MARYLAND

VIRGINIA

*The Ohio Valley in the 1750s*

● *French trading posts and forts*  *Established French trade routes* ◄

● *English trading posts and forts*  *English traders moving west* ◄

*George Washington*

The French and the English both wanted to control this important area. The French saw the Ohio Valley as the gateway to the West, while the English viewed it as rich and fertile farmland. After land was granted to the Ohio Company of Virginia in 1749 by George II, English explorers, settlers, and traders began to move into the Ohio Valley. The French, alarmed by the English claims and advances, prepared to defend what they considered to be French territory. They added to the long chain of forts that now ran from the Great Lakes to the Forks of the Ohio, where the Allegheny and Monongahela Rivers met to form the Ohio River.

In 1753, the English sent the first of two expeditions into the Ohio Valley under the command of a young army major named George Washington. He was to oversee the building of a small fort near the Forks and to warn the French to leave English territory—a warning the French ignored. The following year, Washington returned with one hundred fifty men and led an attack on a small patrol, killing a number of French soldiers.

From their newly built Fort Duquesne, the French planned revenge. They put together a huge force and took off after the Virginians. To protect themselves, Washington and his men built a small stockade they called Fort Necessity. When nine hundred French soldiers and Indian warriors attacked from the wooded hillsides, the small fort did not hold. Washington was forced to surrender, but the French allowed him an honorable retreat. The major and the other survivors marched home to Virginia.

With their long string of forts and their many loyal Indian allies, the French were in an ideal position to hold the Ohio Valley. Most Indians did not believe in risking human life unnecessarily in battles that could not be won, so they were most willing to help their French friends when they saw the possibility of victory. Other tribes, who did not count the French as friends, still saw them as the lesser of two evils and often sided with them against the English.

*Fort Duquesne*

The English knew that they could never win against the French without Indian help. Important colonial leaders, including Benjamin Franklin of Philadelphia, organized a big meeting in 1754. They invited more than one hundred Iroquois chiefs to attend. They hoped to enlist their support once again in the ongoing struggle with the French. Promises were made, and many wagonloads of gifts were given to help seal the agreement. The colonists came away feeling that they could truly rely on the Iroquois in the years ahead.

At the same meeting, Franklin proposed a plan to organize the colonies into a union for their common defense. Although most of the delegates approved, the proposal was later rejected by the individual colonial governments, whose members were afraid that the alliance would take away their independence.

*Benjamin Franklin*

The following year, the British sent General Edward Braddock to America to command the British regulars, or professional soldiers. His mission was to reach the Ohio Valley and take Fort Duquesne from the French. With a combined force of about two thousand redcoats, as the British troops were called, and colonial militiamen, Braddock led a slow formal march through a wilderness of dense forest. In front of the four-mile-long column, axmen tirelessly worked to clear a road on which the soldiers could travel. As only a few miles could be cleared each day, the journey took many weeks.

*General Braddock*

*A fife-and-drum corps leads Braddock's men toward the Ohio Valley.*

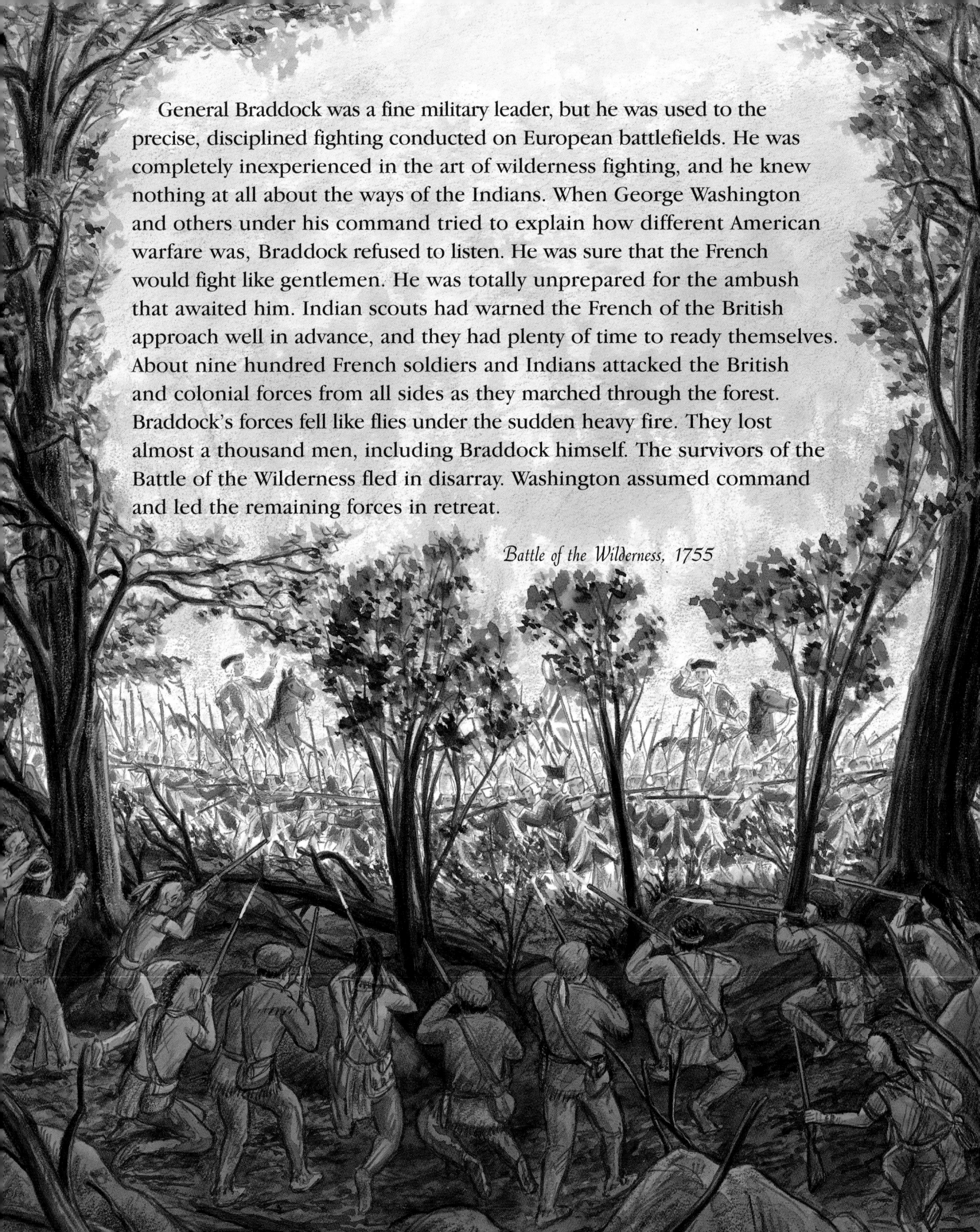

General Braddock was a fine military leader, but he was used to the precise, disciplined fighting conducted on European battlefields. He was completely inexperienced in the art of wilderness fighting, and he knew nothing at all about the ways of the Indians. When George Washington and others under his command tried to explain how different American warfare was, Braddock refused to listen. He was sure that the French would fight like gentlemen. He was totally unprepared for the ambush that awaited him. Indian scouts had warned the French of the British approach well in advance, and they had plenty of time to ready themselves. About nine hundred French soldiers and Indians attacked the British and colonial forces from all sides as they marched through the forest. Braddock's forces fell like flies under the sudden heavy fire. They lost almost a thousand men, including Braddock himself. The survivors of the Battle of the Wilderness fled in disarray. Washington assumed command and led the remaining forces in retreat.

*Battle of the Wilderness, 1755*

*Iroquois leaders meet with the British at the home of William Johnson.*

*William Johnson*

The British had suffered a terrible defeat—they had lost men and supplies, as well as the respect of many colonists and Indians. They now hoped for victories in other regions of North America to reclaim their honor, and they looked for help and advice from those who knew the Indians and were skilled in wilderness fighting. William Johnson, an Irish-born fur trader who lived in Iroquois country in New York, had for years been on excellent terms with the Mohawk. He put together an army of militiamen and Indians to fight the French wilderness-style. His forces helped the British take the French forts on Lake Champlain.

After two years of fighting in America, Britain officially declared war on France in 1756, and the conflict quickly spread around the globe.

At first, British victories were few and far between in the French and Indian War—the last in this series of wars and the only one actually called by that name in America. The French had a brilliant new general, the Marquis de Montcalm. One of his allies, an Ottawa chief, was said to have been surprised at how small Montcalm was. But when he looked into the French leader's eyes, the chief proclaimed that he saw "the strength and greatness of the pine tree and the spirit and courage of the eagle." The young general soon led the French to a series of victories, taking British forts on Lake Ontario and Lake George. It seemed that the French were on their way to final victory in North America.

*The Marquis de Montcalm*       *Lord Jeffrey Amherst*       *General James Wolfe*

But the British were not ready to give up the fight. The government in England, under a new prime minister—William Pitt—decided to put greater effort into winning the war in America. Money, equipment, and troops poured into the American colonies. Pitt also sent a number of new leaders, including Lord Jeffrey Amherst and Brigadier General James Wolfe, to challenge Montcalm and manage the military effort against the French.

In 1758, in a huge, well-planned attack, they took Louisbourg once more from the French. Other French forts began to fall, and the British captured Fort Duquesne in the Ohio Valley. It was renamed Fort Pitt and would later be the site of the city of Pittsburgh. But these victories were marred by one terrible defeat that same year, at Fort Ticonderoga on Lake Champlain in New York. In two separate attacks, the British lost almost two thousand men and were forced to flee southward.

*The British and Indian encampment at Lake George,*
*New York, under French attack in 1755*

The following year, William Johnson and Iroquois warriors aided the redcoats in capturing Fort Niagara on Lake Ontario. But the biggest battle in all the French and Indian Wars was yet to be waged—the battle for Québec. The British had always known that to truly defeat the French, they would have to take the city of Québec, the very heart of New France. This would be the most difficult challenge of all, one that had defeated them twice before. The center of the city sat atop cliff walls that rose two hundred feet above the St. Lawrence River. The seemingly impossible task of penetrating this French stronghold was left to General Wolfe. He positioned his force of nine thousand men and his huge fleet of ships below Québec. Wolfe needed to find a way to force the French out from behind the walls of the city, but first he had to get his army up the steep cliffs.

*Under cover of darkness, Wolfe's ships sail west past Québec.*

For a number of months, while his artillery fired upon the city day and night, Wolfe searched for a solution. At last, he located a narrow path west of the city that was not well guarded. During the night, more than four thousand of his men struggled up to the top of the cliff. By dawn, they were ready and assembled for battle on the Plains of Abraham—a large field just outside the city walls.

Montcalm had hoped to wait the British out until winter ice forced them to withdraw, but now, ready or not, he was forced to face Wolfe, and defend Québec from British attack. He knew he had not a moment to waste—more British troops were waiting below. Montcalm ordered his army to emerge from the protection of the city walls and take their place on the battlefield.

*British soldiers ascending the cliffs*

The British waited—holding their ground, not firing—as the French advanced toward them. At about one hundred yards, the French opened fire, but the British held back until their enemy was only forty yards away. Then the French fell quickly under heavy attack from muskets and bayonets.

The battle had taken months to plan, but it was over in just minutes. Wolfe died on the battlefield. His last words were: "God be praised, I will die in peace." Montcalm, too, died of his wounds a short time later. When told that all was lost, he answered, "So much the better. I will not see the surrender of Québec."

Four days later, Québec was surrendered to the British. The following summer, Montréal fell too, and with it, all of New France.

*The Battle of Québec, 1759*

The Treaty of Paris, ending the war, was signed in 1763. Under its terms, all French territory in North America went to the British, except for Louisiana, which was given to Spain. Spain in turn agreed to give up Florida to the English. English forces gloried in their victory and quickly moved west to take over the French forts on the Great Lakes and in other areas.

But the English were caught off guard by the reaction of the Indians. Many tribes loyal to the French were surprised by the British takeover. They had not expected a French defeat, and now they looked to the British for the same protection, supplies, and favors they had readily received from their French friends. But Lord Amherst, who was now in charge, did not approve of the French way. He ordered the Indians out of the French forts and settlements and refused to resupply them with the ammunition and goods they had come to depend on.

The Indians were furious at this cold treatment. Pontiac, an Ottawa chief and faithful ally of the French, led a rebellion against the British, and many tribes rose to fight with him. Over the next three years, English forts and settlements again came under attack, this time by the Indians alone. At first, the revolution was very successful. But in the end, the Indians lacked the unity and resources to force the English out. The Indians expected French support, which never came. In 1766, Pontiac was forced to agree to peace terms.

In the years ahead, the Indians would be forced to accept many more concessions from the new Americans, who were constantly pushing westward. Although British officials had promised the Indians that no settlement would be allowed west of the Allegheny Mountains, within a few years that promise, as well as many others, would be broken by colonial settlers.

*Pontiac's forces attack Fort Detroit, 1763.*

*Chief Pontiac*

*Colonists stage a protest against British taxes.*

The English colonists had become very independent over the years and weren't always willing to do as they were told by Great Britain. Over many years of self-government, they had become used to a great deal of freedom. Once, they had needed their mother country for supplies and for protection against the French and Spanish. But now, with their enemies defeated and their economy strong, they felt safe and quite able to take care of themselves. Many colonists no longer felt like British citizens—they had begun to think of themselves as Americans.

Now that the colonists were no longer busy thinking of war, they turned to other matters. Still angry over the many trade restrictions that Great Britain had forced on them over the years, they were outraged when England decided that the colonies should help pay for the last war through a series of new taxes.

The English victory in North America would be short-lived. Already the spirit of independence and rebellion was spreading throughout the colonies. Great Britain would soon be led into another war—this time against her own colonies. And that day was not far away.

# Additional Information
## More About Colonial America: 1689–1763

### Freedom of the Press

In 1734, John Peter Zenger, publisher of *The Weekly Journal,* was arrested for writing articles critical of the colonial government of New York. At his trial in 1735, the jury found him not guilty. This trial helped establish one of the basic freedoms of American democracy—freedom of the press—that would later be guaranteed by the Constitution.

### Peace Pipes

Large tobacco pipes were smoked at many important Native American ceremonies. The pipe bowls were made of polished stone; the long stems were made of wood and often decorated with feathers. The French adopted the custom of sitting in a circle and passing the pipe with their Indian trading partners, and the pipes came to be called calumets, from the French word *chalumeaux,* meaning *flutes* or *tubes.* They were often referred to as peace pipes, even though they were used in all important decision-making, including declarations of war.

### Health and Medicine

There were few real doctors in colonial times, and little was known about disease prevention, so epidemics of diseases such as smallpox were common. In 1721, during a smallpox outbreak in Boston, a well-known minister, Cotton Mather, persuaded Dr. Zabdiel Boylston to administer injections of pus from sick individuals to more than two hundred Bostonians. These inoculations marked the beginning of disease prevention and public health care in the American colonies. Although many in Boston thought inoculation was a kind of witchcraft, the idea caught on, and by 1776 the practice was fairly common.

### Elizabeth Lucas

In 1741, nineteen-year-old Elizabeth Lucas (later Pinckney) introduced the cultivation of the indigo plant to South Carolina. By 1744, her first successful indigo crop was shipped to England, where the deep blue dye produced by the plant was very popular. Lucas distributed seeds to other planters, and by the 1760s, the colony sold a million pounds of dye a year to England.

### Money

The first copper coins in the colonies were minted in Simsbury, Connecticut, in 1737. They were produced by John Higley, and so were called Higley pennies. They were stamped with two sayings: "I am good copper" on one side, and "Value me as you will" on the other. Since money was not the same from colony to colony, the value could be decided by the users. Any object of value—tobacco, for instance—could be used as money, as well.

### Salem Witch Trials

In 1692, a group of young girls in Salem, Massachusetts, falsely accused a slave of being a witch. In Puritan times, most people believed in witches and feared them greatly. Panic and suspicion caused mass hysteria in Salem, and soon the jail was filled with more than one hundred accused witches. Trials were held, and many innocent victims were found guilty. Over a period of about four months, twenty "witches" were executed. Finally, reason was restored, and those suspects still in jail were released. In 1697, an official apology was offered, and some payments were made to the families of those who had been put to death.

### Almanacs

In colonial America, the publishing of books, newspapers, and other reading matter was a thriving business. One especially popular type of publication was the almanac. The name comes from an Arabic word, *al-manakh,* meaning a timetable of the skies—a kind of heavenly calendar. The first in the American colonies, called *An Almanack for New England,* was published in 1639. "Weather, Wit, and Wisdom" were the main features of these yearly publications. They contained advice for farmers, records, and information about the weather and tides, household hints, recipes, and tips for good health. Benjamin Franklin began publishing his *Poor Richard's Almanac* in 1732. The familiar *Old Farmer's Almanac,* still read today, first appeared in 1793.

### Benjamin Bannecker

Born in Maryland in 1731, to a recently freed Black family, Benjamin Bannecker was allowed to attend a local school, where he proved to be an excellent student. Although farming was his main occupation, he was an accomplished amateur astronomer and mathematician, as well as a publisher and inventor. At the age of thirty, he constructed the first striking clock in the colonies to be made entirely of American parts. His clock kept perfect time for forty years, striking every hour. Later in his life, Bannecker, who was much admired by Thomas Jefferson, helped survey the land for Washington, D.C.

### Population

In 1690, the population in the English colonies stood at about 213,500. By 1760, the number had swelled to 1,600,000, about 80 percent of whom were European and 20 percent, African. The number of French colonists stood at fewer than 80,000. As the population of the English colonies grew, the number of Native Americans decreased. While there were certainly hundreds of thousands of Indians living in North America, no one knows what the exact number was in 1690 or in 1760.

# Exploration and Explorers 1689–1763

As the population in the colonies grew, more and more settlers wanted to move west, where there was more open land. English companies such as the Hudson Bay Company sent explorers to map and lay claim to new areas, but opening new territories for settlement was a dangerous and risky business. The Indians and the French claimed most of the land beyond the English colonial borders and actively resisted those they viewed as intruders. However, despite the dangers, England, Spain, and France continued to encourage further exploration into the interior. The Spanish began to move west along the Gulf Coast from Florida and north from Mexico into what would later be Texas and New Mexico. Russia sent explorers into North America, as well—in 1741, Vitus Bering sailed to the Gulf of Alaska and the Aleutian Islands. These are some of the many explorers of the period:

1690–1692 *Henry Kelsey* (English) travels from Hudson Bay to the Canadian plains.

1699–1700 *Pierre Le Moyne, Sieur d'Iberville*, and his brother *Jean-Baptiste Le Moyne, Sieur de Bienville* (French), explore the Mississippi Delta.

1700–1702 *Pierre Le Sueur* (French) travels up the Mississippi River into Minnesota.

1716–1720 *Domingo Ramon, Hernando de Alarcon* (Spanish) and others lead expeditions from Mexico into what is now Texas, New Mexico, and Louisiana.

1738–1753 The *Verendryes: Pierre Gaultier de Varennes de Sieur* (French) and his three sons explore the upper Missouri River, and from Lake Superior to the Saskatchewan River.

1739–1741 *Paul* and *Pierre Mallet* (French) travel from New Orleans to the Great Plains and southwest into what is now New Mexico.

1742 *John Peter Salley* and *John Howard* (English) explore the Blue Ridge Mountains of Virginia and continue westward to the Mississippi River.

1750 *Dr. Thomas Walker* (English) reaches the Cumberland Gap, gateway to Kentucky.

1750–1752 *Christopher Gist* and *John Finley* (English) explore the Ohio River and Kentucky.

1754–1755 *Anthony Henday* (English) travels from Hudson Bay to the lower Saskatchewan River.

# More About the Iroquois League

Many years before European explorers came to North America, possibly as early as the 1400s, the Five Nations of the Iroquois Confederacy joined forces to bring about peace and increase their power. The union gave them protection from outside enemies while ensuring peaceful relations among themselves. Each of the five nations was independent and self-governing, but once a year, they sent representatives to a council where they discussed matters of concern to all, such as warfare and trade. After open discussion, a vote was taken on each issue. Each nation agreed to accept and follow any agreement reached by the council. A number of ideas from the Iroquois system of government were borrowed by the framers of the American Constitution.

# More About Benjamin Franklin

Benjamin Franklin was born in Boston in 1706. He moved to Philadelphia as a young man, where he was so successful at his business of publishing, printing, and bookselling that he was able to retire in 1743 at the age of thirty-seven. During the rest of his life, Franklin was a scientist, writer, scholar, inventor, statesman, and diplomat. Among his inventions were the lightning rod, bifocal glasses, and the Franklin stove. He reorganized the colonial postal system and helped found the Philadelphia police and fire departments, the first public library and hospital, and the University of Pennsylvania. In his later years, he served in colonial government and as an ambassador to both England and France. Franklin died in 1790, at the age of eighty-four.

# Index

Page numbers in *italics* refer to illustrations.

almanacs, 46
Amherst, Lord Jeffrey, 39, *39, 43*

Baltimore, 31, *31*
Bannecker, Benjamin, 46
Beaver Wars, 9
Blacks, 21, *21,* 46
Boston, *14,* 20, 28, 30
Braddock, Edward, 35–36, *35*

Carolinas, 13, 21, 23, 25, 30
Charleston, 20, *20–21,* 23

Deerfield (Massachusetts), 22, *22*
Detroit, 18, *19,* 44, *44*
Dutch, the, 4, 9

English settlements, 5, 13, *13, 16,* 19–21,
    *19, 20,* 25, *25,* 26, 31, *31,* 46
  tax revolt by, 45, *45*
explorers, 47

Five Nations, 7, 47
Fort Duquesne, *32–33,* 33, 35, 39
Fort Necessity, *32–33,* 33
Fort Niagara, 40
Fort Ticonderoga, 39
Franklin, Benjamin, 34, *34,* 47
freedom of the press, 46
French and Indian Wars, 14–17, *14–16,* 22–23,
    *22, 23,* 26, 28–29, *28–29,* 32–43, *34–43*
French settlements, 5, *12,* 15, *17,* 18, 20, 24,
    *24, 26, 26,* 31
fur trade, 4, 8–10, *8,* 15, 18, 19

Georgia, 25, *25*
Great Lakes, 4, *4,* 15, 19, 24, 32, *32,* 43

Hudson Bay Company, *19,* 47
Hudson River and Valley, 9, 15
Huguenots, 20

Indians
  Algonquian tribes, 6–9, *6, 7, 9,* 11–13,
    25, 34, *37,* 40
  early wars of, 8, 9, *9,* 11
  after French defeat, 43–44, *44,* 46
  Iroquoian tribes, 6–9, *6, 7, 9,* 11–13, 25,
    34, *37,* 40, 47
  map of, *6*
  peace pipes of, 46
  as slaves, 21, 25
  trade goods of, 10–11, *11*
  tribal identity of, 11
  *See also* French and Indian Wars

Jamestown, 8
Johnson, William, 37, *37,* 40

King George's War, 26, 28–29, *28–29*
King William's War, 16–17, *16*

Lachine (Canada), 15
Lake Champlain, 16, 24, 26, 37
Lake George encampment, *38–39,* 39
Louisbourg, 24, *24,* 26, *26–29,* 28–29, 39

maps, *4, 6, 14, 18*
Mohawk tribe, 7, 37
money, 46
Montcalm, Marquis de, 39, *39,* 41–42
Moravians, 31, *31*

Native Americans. *See* Indians
naval battle, *3*
New England, 8, 13, 17, *20,* 21, 22, 26, 28–29
New Orleans, 31
New York City, *13,* 20

Oglethorpe, James, 25
Ohio Valley, 31–36, *32*
Ottawa tribe, 8, 44

Philadelphia, 20, 34
Pittsburgh, 39
Plymouth, 8
Pontiac, 44, *44*
population
  English, 5, 13, 20
  French, 5, 12
  Indian, 6
Port Royal, 17, *17,* 23

Québec, 14, 17, *17,* 23
  1759 battle for, 40–42, *40–43*
Queen Anne's War, 22–23, *22, 23*

religious intolerance, 22

Saint Lawrence River, 4, *4, 12,* 15, 17, 23–24,
    40, *40*
Salem witch trials, 46
Savannah, 25, *25*
Schenectady, 16, *16*
slavery, 21, *21,* 25
smallpox, 46
Spanish, the, 4, *4,* 18, *18,* 23, 25, 31, 43

trade, 10–15, 20, 25, 45
  fur, 4, 8–10, *8,* 15, 18, 19
trade goods, 10–11, *11*
transportation, 30, *30*
Treaty of Paris (1763), 43
Tuscarora tribe, 25

Virginia, 13, 30, 32–33

Washington, George, 32, *32,* 36, 46
Wilderness, Battle of the, 36
Wolfe, James, 39–42, *39*

Yamasee tribe, 25

Zenger, John Peter, 46